Arthur Featherstone Marshall

Reply to the Bishop of Ripon's Attack on the Catholic Church

Arthur Featherstone Marshall

Reply to the Bishop of Ripon's Attack on the Catholic Church

ISBN/EAN: 9783337162627

Printed in Europe, USA, Canada, Australia, Japan

Cover: Foto ©ninafisch / pixelio.de

More available books at **www.hansebooks.com**

TO

THE BISHOP OF RIPON'S ATTACK

ON

THE CATHOLIC CHURCH.

BY A LAYMAN.

Τὸ σχίσμα ὑμῶν πολλοὺς διέστρεψεν, πολλοὺς εἰς ἀθυμίαν
ἔβαλεν, πολλοὺς εἰς δισταγμὸν, τοὺς πάντας ἡμᾶς εἰς
λύπην· καὶ ἐπίμονος ὑμῶν ἐστιν ἡ στάσις.

St. Clement's First Epistle to the Corinthians.

PUBLISHED BY

THE SHEFFIELD CATHOLIC ASSOCIATION, 20, PARADISE SQUARE,

SHEFFIELD.

1874.

Imprimatur.

✠ ROBERTUS EPISCOPUS BEVERLACENSIS.

The Bishop of Ripon has preached a Sermon in his Cathedral against the errors of the Catholic Church. His Lordship's sermon is the most satisfactory answer to the positions which he himself takes up. He says that "mistakes in religion may lead to consequences fatal to the soul's salvation;" and then he proceeds to revile that sole authority which can prevent men from making mistakes. He speaks of "the necessity of some fixed standard of appeal;" and then argues that no such standard of appeal is to be found on the face of the earth. He asks, "Whom can we trust?" And then, having stated that we cannot trust the Church, he shows conspicuously that we cannot trust *him*. "Human opinions are proverbially uncertain and fluctuating," very truthfully observes his Lordship; after which he goes on to elaborately prove that Protestant opinions are human. This is the sort of reasoning to which we are daily accustomed from the modern apostles of Protestantism. It is no fault of the Bishop that he cannot discourse upon authority without being inconsistent and illogical; because his position obliges him to make assertions which are negatived by sense and by fact. To be a Protestant is to be necessarily inconsistent; nor can we help feeling compassion for the champions of a heresy which is without parallel in the kingdom of fallacies.

To attempt to "answer" the Bishop would be to attempt to write a book; since he touches on a score of different subjects—every one of them involving much thought. It will suffice that we merely sketch the kind of criticism we should offer, were we gravely to undertake such a task.

The Bishop breaks a lance with tradition; not seeing that in doing so he is really undermining his own position as an Anglican Protestant. He will have it that traditions, apostolical and ecclesiastical, are comparatively of very little importance; while he himself would interpret every word of the Scriptures solely by his Protestant traditions. He speaks of those traditions in the Catholic Church which "plainly contradict God's Word;" the extreme plainness of their contradiction being found in the fact that the whole Catholic Church thinks the contrary. Moreover, the Greek Church, and many Oriental sects, hold that the "plainness" of these very doctrines of Scripture is in their sense of acceptation, not the Bishop's. He says that "the greater part of these peculiar dogmas of the Roman Catholic Church"—which, however, with the exception of two or three, are also the peculiar dogmas of the Greek Church—"rest upon the authority of tradition, and tradition alone;" whereas every Catholic child, who has been properly instructed, can quote chapter and verse for every dogma. And here the Bishop gives a forcible illustration of the utter untenableness of his theory. He admits that the change of the Sabbath, from the seventh to the first day of the week, is certainly a matter of tradition; but he gets over this by asserting that "the essence of the observance is the same, whether it be the first day of the week or the seventh." Was there ever a more unwarrantable assumption? So that it belongs to us to teach God what is the "essence" of His Commandments, and it belongs to Him to obey our instructions. Of course, every Catholic knows that the Church has no power to change one iota of God's Commandments; and that it is solely because the apostolic tradition is of equal weight with the Gospels and the Epistles, that therefore the Church accepts that tradition, as conveying the unwritten word. In those forty days when our Lord was upon earth, after He had risen from the dead, as well as upon those innumerable occasions when, before His death, He was

alone with His Apostles, it is certain that He gave
secret instructions to the Apostles, which instructions
are but shadowed in the Scriptures. The Church, being
the inspired mistress of truth, is the sole keeper and
interpreter of these traditions. She cannot go wrong
in regard of the traditions, because she has the Holy
Spirit to guide her. If the Church could teach the
smallest fragment of heresy, in regard of the written or
the unwritten Word, she would be human, like Protestantism, a pretender and imposter, worthy of nothing
but contempt. But the Bishop of Ripon affirms of the
Church that she is a human—that, is a fallible—institu- .
tion, and yet that she may change God's Commandments.
He says that it belongs to man to decide what is the
" essence " of a commandment ; and that though God
commanded the seventh day to be kept, man has the
right to keep the first. Man has not the right to do
any such thing. Unless the Apostolic tradition in
regard of the change of the day rest upon a divine
Commandment, the change of the day is impiety ; and
since it is from tradition alone that we know of the
commandment, it follows that the tradition is of God.
In other words, if the tradition is *not* Apostolic, the
Commandment can *not* be of force. And we have no
means of judging of the apostolicity of the tradition,
save only the authority of the Church. We do not see
how to evade the conclusion.*

Here pass we for a moment to another statement
of the Bishop, which is sympathetic in position with the
last. The Bishop finds fault with the Catholic Rule of
Faith,—without however substituting another ; and

---

* The late Rev. John Keble preached a sermon in Winchester Cathedral, during the year
1837, on the importance of the Apostolical Tradition. Taking for his text the words : " That good
thing which was committed unto thee keep by the Holy Ghost that dwelleth in us," Mr. Keble
thus lucidly reasoned :—
    " If we will be impartial, we cannot hide from ourselves that His Unwritten Word, if it can
be anyhow authenticated, must necessarily demand the same reverence from us as His Written
Word ; and for the very same reason, because it is His Word. . . . I do not see how we can be
wrong in inferring, from these and similar passages," (Mr. Keble had been quoting such passages as,
" Wherefore, brethren, stand fast, and hold the traditions ye have been taught, whether by word
or our epistle ") " that the faith once for all delivered to the Saints, in other words, Apostolical
Tradition, was divinely appointed in the Church as the touchstone of Canonical Scripture itself. . .
I need hardly remind you of the unquestioned historical fact, that the very Nicene Creed itself, to
which perhaps of all formulæ we are most indebted for a sound belief in a proper Divinity of the

urges that practically, the Catholic rule of faith renders the Scriptures a dead letter:

> "The Roman Catholic, whoever he may be, is forbidden to interpret a single verse of Scripture except as the Church has interpreted it, and except as he finds it to be according to the unanimous consent of the fathers. But I say without hesitation that the unanimous consent of the fathers is a phantom which eludes every attempt to reach it. You can never discover it. You can never possibly find where it is. You can never be sure that you have that unanimous consent, without which the Church of Rome prohibits you to interpret a single verse of God's Holy Word."

All this we should be disposed to agree to, in the sense in which the Bishop intends it. It is absolutely impossible for any private individual to form complete, infallible appreciation of all the teaching of all the Fathers on all doctrines. But this is not what the Church means to teach. What the Church teaches is this: that a consensus of the Fathers on any given doctrine is a determining point in her teaching; and that since the Church is the sole mistress of truth, it belongs to her to interpret the Fathers. Here and there a Father might be wrong; as where St. Cyprian got wrong upon Baptism, but subsequently submitted to right teaching. In such case, the Church, being judge of all doctrine, would correct a doctor where he might happen to be in error, and he would submit to the Church. Where the Church has not defined a particular truth, it is open to theologians to discuss it; but where the Vicar of God has set his seal on a truth,

---

Son of God, even this Creed had its origin, not from Scripture, but from tradition. The 300 Bishops who joined in the promulgation did not profess to have collected it out of the Bible, but simply to express the faith—which each of them had found in the Church which he represented—received by tradition from the Apostles. . . The very writings of the Apostles were to be tried first by tradition, before they could be incorporated into the canon. Thus the Scriptures themselves, as it were, do homage to the tradition of the Apostles; and despisers therefore of that tradition take part, inadvertently or profanely, with the despisers of the Scripture itself."

The Bishop of Ripon says that tradition is condemned "ten times" in the Bible. We know not to what passages he alludes. But certain it is that where tradition is condemned; as certain as that, where it is true, it is approved. There must be false traditions, as there must be false prophets, false churches, false priests, false bishops.

there is an end for ever of discussion. The Fathers
were the first to recognise this principle, the first to
submit where there had been margin for controversy,
but where *now* there was no province but to obey. St.
Cyprian is one of the happiest of examples. " All
heresies and schisms," he energetically teaches, " have
sprung from a disregard of the one Priest and Judge,
to whom Christ has delegated His power. For if, in
compliance with the instructions of our Lord, every
member of the Christian community yielded a docile
obedience to the Representative of God, the unity of the
Church would never be rent." This was the teaching
of him who had differed, though but temporarily, from
the spirit of the Church. So that a " consensus of the
Fathers " must be always taken as meaning a consensus
allowed by the Church; since the grains of false teaching,
among the bushels of truth, must be winnowed by
inspired authority. But the position of the Bishop—
that because it is impossible for individuals to detect
these small grains for themselves, therefore it must be
impossible for the Church—is a position which, while
true in its first part, is lamentably false in its second.
Truth is a deposit in the Church, it is subject to the
attacks of human craftiness, and must sometimes be
opposed by even heresy; but it is just here that the
Church has her mission, to separate the wheat from the
chaff. Most true is that remark of the Bishop—that
for every Catholic to be obliged to wade through
decretals of Popes, folios of bulls and of councils,
endless chronicles of the disputes of the schoolmen, is
a thing so utterly impracticable, that if the rule of faith
imposed such a condition, it would impose what scarcely
any could perform. But the Church does not require
anything of the kind. She says to her people: I am
the mistress of truth; and when I teach, I am preserved
from being deceived; therefore trust to Me to do for you
what you cannot do for yourselves; since the promises
are made to Me, not to you.—But see here what confusion the Bishop encounters, in denying the Catholic

rule of faith. The Church is not competent to fix the teaching of the Fathers—so says the Bishop of Ripon—but Protestants are competent, each one for himself, to fix the whole teaching of the Scripture. The Church is not competent to decide what the Bible teaches, any more than to decide what the Fathers taught; but every Protestant is competent to judge the Bible and the Fathers, to summon both to the bar of his opinions.—And at this point we would call attention to one of the broadest illustrations of the hopeless fallacy of this position. We know that High Churchmen affect to obey the Fathers; that they boast obedience to that now silent voice, which they imagine they still perfectly understand. They interpret the Scriptures by the Fathers; they judge the Church of England by the early Church; they submit, or they rebel, according to their private interpretation of certain writings of certain primitive authors. These men, then, do that for themselves, which the Bishop says the Catholic Church is utterly incompetent to do for them. They are the self-constituted authorities to judge the Catholic Church, the writings of every one of the ancients, the Church of England, the Greek Church, the Bible, ecclesiastical history, and tradition. More than this, they judge all living authorities, throughout the whole of professing Christendom.—But the Bishop of Ripon belongs perhaps to another school. He takes what he calls the Bible for his rule; that is, he takes his private interpretation, for his sole guide in faith and in morals. Now it is obvious that the main difference between the rule of faith of Low Churchmen and the rule of faith of High Churchmen or Ritualists is that Low Churchmen limit their popedom to the Bible, whereas the others extend it over antiquity. Both take themselves as sole interpreters of their teachers; only each elects his teacher for himself, before he proceeds to judge him. This is practically shown in that passage of the Bishop's sermon, where he treats of the " Apocryphal " Scriptures :

" Blended with the Scriptures in the Roman

Catholic rule of faith, there is the Apocrypha. We of the Church of England altogether object to placing the Apocrypha on a level with the inspired Word of God. The Jews, from whom we received it, never regarded the Apocrypha as inspired at all. The books of the Apocrypha were not written in pure Hebrew. They are never once quoted by our Lord, or by the Apostles in the New Testament. For the first four centuries of the Christian Church they were not received as forming any part of the inspired Word of God. They do not claim to be inspired, and they teach doctrines which are repugnant to God's Word. From the Apocrypha you may defend suicide, you may defend lying, you may defend purgatory, you may defend salvation by works. We object on these grounds to allow the Apocrypha to be placed on a level with the Word of God, as forming any part whatever of that rule of faith by which our religious belief is to be guided and determined."

Now the Bishop forgets that he authorises his clergy to read the "Apocrypha" in their churches; consequently, "lying," and "purgatory," and "salvation by works," might be urged on the authority of the Bishop. Moreover, the Church of England, of which the Bishop is a pillar, affirms that the Church reads the Apocrypha "for example of life and instruction in manners;" so that the Bishop has the misfortune to differ from his Church on the real character and merit of these books. Perhaps he will tell us that some parts of the Apocrypha are true, while others are distressingly false. Well, to judge one's own teachers is so essentially a principle of the whole system of "Protestant Christianity," that we can never be surprised at any example of its practice which we meet with in the history of that sect. Yet it must be remembered that the "Apocryphal" writings are vouched for, in regard of their inspiration, by the *same* authority which vouches for the Gospels ; so that if the Church be wrong in regard of the Apocrypha, she may be wrong in regard of the Gospels. It was not until the end of the fourth century that the canon of the Scriptures was fixed ; the third Council of Carthage and a decretal of Pope Innocent being the authorities which set the matter at rest. Before that time, numerous Apocryphal prophecies, as well as numerous Apocryphal gospels and epistles, had found more or less favour with the learned ; some insisting on the authenticity of books which at Carthage were pronounced to be spurious ; others rejecting some of the really inspired books which at Carthage were pronounced to be genuine. And it is at this point we would ask a question of Protestants, which it very seriously concerns them to answer. If the same authority which gave judgment on the Epistle to the Hebrews, and on six other books of the New Testament, gave judgment on the canonicity of the Apocrypha, how comes it that this judgment is binding in the one case, but is not binding in the other ? If the same authority which decreed the canonicity of " Revelations," and of five books in particular of the Old Testament, decreed also the canonicity of ' Judith ' and ' Tobias,'—which, we presume, the Bishop of Ripon rejects,—why accept the authority in regard of the former, but reject it in regard of the latter ? Is it not manifest that if the Church was not infallible on a part, she could not be infallible on the whole ; or, conversely, that if the Church was not infallible on the whole, she could not be infallible on a part ? Either accept the infallibility of the Church, as settling the canon of the Scriptures ; or reject it,—and then away goes authority, and all possibility of knowing the truth.

But we cannot leave this subject without still further investigating the rationale of the Christian's rule of faith.

There needs no argument to show that without an external authority—an authority external to the Scriptures—canonicity can never be vouched ; since it would be simply absurd to say that the Scriptures guarantee their own limits or exactness. Take one example out of many. The Church of England has rejected the Epistle of St. Barnabas, who is called "Apostle" and "full of the Holy Ghost," but has accepted the Gospels of St. Mark and St. Luke who were not of the number of the Apostles. On what authority has she ventured to do this? Is she plenarily inspired to set apart an apostle, and to throne in his place a disciple? Or is she plenarily inspired, in this nineteenth century, to know whether an epistle was really written by St. Barnabas, or by some one affecting his name? She cannot possibly know anything about it. The time is too far back to summon data to our aid; to judge a matter that was long since out of court. So again: What warrant have Protestants for positively asserting that certain books were really written by certain authors; that Phebe did not alter the Epistle to the Romans, or Tychicus the Epistle to the Ephesians; that all the Gospels and all the Epistles, in size, words, and stops, are what they were when they issued from their authors? They have positively no warrant whatever. The Epistle to the Hebrews—like many other of the Epistles—was from the earliest times subjected to doubt; so that Origen could only write: "If I were to give my opinion, I should say that the thoughts are the Apostle's, but that the wording and construction are the work of some one else." Thus, take away the infallibility of the Church, her infallibility in judging tradition, and you take away the certainty of the canonicity of those Scriptures which have been volumed for many hundreds of years. As the Archbishop of Westminster has observed: "The schism which rent England from the Divine Tradition of Faith rent it also from the source of certainty." And so profoundly has this truth been realised by many of the most erudite Anglicans, that they have gone so far as to admit the infallibility of the *earlier* Councils of the Church. They have felt that the creeds would be worth nothing at all, unless the authority was infallible which compiled them ; and that an infallible canon is an absolute impossibility, without an infallible Church to decide it. It was argued by Hooker, and admitted by Chillingworth, that the Scriptures cannot bear testimony to themselves ; that is, to the range, to the complement, of the "Bible." We are at the mercy of tradition, judged by the Church ; and without tradition and the Church we are nowhere. "I should not believe the Gospel itself," wrote St. Augustine, "if the authority of the Church did not oblige me to do so." And he only wrote what common sense must approve. Yet there still remains the question which it is impossible to answer—but which must be answered by every Protestant: "If the Church was infallible when she decreed the canon, why is she not infallible still ?"

While, if from the difficulties of the canon, we come to those of the translations, there is plenty to make Protestants unhappy. The translations of Tindal, of Coverdale, of Queen Elizabeth's Bishops, were so dangerously corrupt and misleading, that a new version was ordered by King James ; and there are learned persons in our own day who contend that the last version is replete with even serious faults.

And, if from the translations we advance to the interpretations,—what a maze, what chaos is here ; confusion compared to which the confusion of Babel was serenest unanimity and concord. So that it comes to this, to put the matter very briefly : Protestants have three difficulties to get over, before they can make good their theory. (1) If the Church was not infallible when she decreed the Canon of the Scriptures, we have only a fallible Canon ; and if the Church was infallible when she decreed the Canon she must be infallible still. (2) The translation of the Scriptures is a question of scholarship ; and not one person in ten thousand is a scholar. (3) The interpretation of the Scriptures is a most critical matter, more critical even than the translation. So that the Canon, the translation, the interpretation, of the Scriptures form three great difficulties for the Protestant. Any one of these difficulties must be fatal to his theory: all three make the theory phenomenal.*

Yet one more observation we are forced to make, before leaving this question of Scripture.

Protestants do not sufficiently bear in mind, in their controversies with the Catholic Church, that the reign of the Holy Ghost began at Pentecost,—after our Lord had ascended into Heaven. If they bore this in mind, they would not mock Church-authority, which is the voice of the Holy Ghost upon earth. It was not long before the time of His crucifixion when our Lord addressed those words to His Apostles: " I have many things to say to you, but you cannot bear them now. Howbeit, when He, the Spirit of Truth, shall come, He shall lead you into all truth." What those "many things" were which our Lord subsequently revealed, or which were revealed by the Spirit of Truth,—but which are not recorded in the Gospels,—we have no (private) ground to conjecture. There are two points to be borne in mind in regard of this fact—the fact of the reign of the Holy Ghost—(1) that much was said to the Apostles which is not written in the Scriptures; (2) that the Holy Ghost is now Guardian of tradition. With regard to the first point, we can of course know but little. Probably the whole doctrine of the Mass, with many a detail of the Sacraments, were taught by our Lord to His Apostles, in those forty days which are scarcely spoken of in the Gospels, but which were not spent in vain on the earth. Whatever was so revealed was prudently handed down, but not cast like " pearls before swine." If it was necessary, in the first ages of

---

* The same difficulties are multiplied in the case of High Churchmen by many others which are equally terrible. They have to judge for themselves:
(1) Which of the Bishops throughout Christendom have been orthodox;
(2) What doctrines did they concurrently testify;
(3) Which of the many episcopal gatherings were really legitimate councils;
(4) Which of their decrees must be accepted;
(5) Where were the Saints right, and where were the Saints wrong; and who were Saints;
(6) Which of the Apostolical Traditions are true; &c., &c.
And, in addition to these difficulties, those we have mentioned above: the Canon, the Translation, the Interpretation, of the Scriptures.

persecution, that the early Christians should veil the Sacraments from the Pagans ; if they were compelled to say Mass in the Catacombs, and to keep back from even Catechumens a portion of those Mysteries which it would have been profanation to proclaim before old Rome ; we can quite understand how secret would be the teaching which the early Christians would pass to one another. The germ of all truth is in the Gospels and Epistles, the substance of all that Christians must believe ; but the precise ritual and adaptation of doctrine is seldom given in the inspired fragments of the New Testament. " He shall guide you into all truth " was that promise which the Catholic Church alone inherits, and which shall belong to her to the end of the world. The reign of the Holy Ghost commenced upon earth when our Lord departed into Heaven ; and that the gates of hell should never prevail against the Church, is the inevitable result of that reign. " The pillar and ground of truth " is only the pillar and ground, because the Holy Ghost reigns perpetually in the Church, to prevent the possibility of error. Outside the Church all is weakness ; human opinion, human conflict—no Teacher ; but inside the Church is the reign of the Holy Ghost, guiding the Church " into *all* truth." Here is the difference between the Church of God, and that human sect which is called the Church of England. It needs an occasional Bishop to deliver private opinions, in order to comfort poor Protestants in their isolation ; for since there is no rule of faith outside the Church, they must put up with the rule of opinions. What the Bishop of Ripon says to-day will be contradicted by his own clergy to-morrow ; but whatever is said is not of the slightest importance, since nothing can be said but opinion. Protestantism is the deification of opinion. It has the plausible pretext of " obeying the Bible ;" which means really obeying oneself.

But to. proceed with our quotations from the sermon. The Bishop says :

"Now what are we to say in regard to tradition ? In the first place, I would observe this, that
in all the early controversies between the heathens
and the Christians, no appeal was ever made to
tradition. The appeal was invariably made to the
Word of God. The Christians were opposed by
the heathen on the ground of their maintaining
doctrines to be found in God's Word, but there was
no allusion whatever to tradition. Next I observe
this, if tradition only reveals what is contained in
God's Word, it is unnecessary; if, on the other
hand, tradition reveals what is repugnant to God's
Word, it ought to be rejected."

Here are a number of statements, not one of which
is sound. That the heathen should not refer to
Christian tradition, in their contests with the teachers of
Christianity, or that the teachers of Christianity should
not refer to such tradition, would appear to be probable
from the fact that such tradition could have very little
weight with the heathen.* As to the statement that "if
tradition only reveals what is contained in God's Word
it is unnecessary," we should beg entirely to differ. The
interpretation of that Word was best understood by the
Apostles and by those who lived with them; and nothing
could be more valuable, next to our Lord's Words themselves, than the Apostolic construction put upon them.
While the statement that " if tradition reveals what is
repugnant to God's Word, it ought to be rejected," is
simply a begging of the whole question ; since the very
point at issue between the Church and heretics is—what
is "repugnant to God's Word?" For example : Catholics
hold that the Catholic dogma of the Real Presence is
taught most literally in the Gospels. Now Catholics are
as good judges, from even the natural point of view, of

Yet everything must depend on what we mean by tradition ; for, of course, until the Gospels
were written,—which was not for many years after the Ascension,—it was absolutely impossible to
refer to them. When "the Lord added to the Church daily such as should be saved," it was not
through the reading of the New Testament ; for the New Testament did not then exist, and, if it
had existed, it could not have been diffused. The truth is, the Apostles converted the heathen
precisely as Catholic missionaries do now—by the authoritative teaching of their divine office,
assisted by the workings of the Holy Ghost.

what construction should be put upon words, as any and every kind of Protestant; to say nothing of their being *in* the Church, and therefore having the teaching of God. "Repugnance," then, is mere personal conception, mere personal bias, in a Protestant; since Catholics hold that the Protestant heresy is repugnant to God's Word and common sense. We repeat that Catholics are intellectually as competent to judge of the question of "repugnance" as are the contending sects of British Protestants. We have the same Scriptures, the same Fathers, the same scholarship; *plus* a good deal that Protestants have not, to wit, the certainty of Apostolic Orders; and we are convinced that the whole of the "repugnance" lies on the side of modern Protestants. So that when the Bishop goes on to remark : "To be consistent with his belief, surely he, the Catholic, ought to reject whatever is revealed by tradition, which plainly contradicts God's Word," we answer that we quite agree with the Bishop ; and that we reject false traditions as much as he does. Only, the very question of what "plainly contradicts God's Word" is exactly the question at issue. It is the conviction of·Catholics that Protestant traditions, on at least a score of Christian obligations, "plainly contradict God's Word;" and it is to them inconceivable how, possessing a Bible, Protestants can maintain such heresies. Catholics open their eyes, in mute wonder and misery, when they hear Protestants propound blank heresies or absurdities which "plainly contradict God's Word." So that the Bishop must remember that he is not the only educated gentleman who has sense and information and scholarship. The Council of Trent was at least as good a judge of what "plainly contradicts God's Word" as any Protestant Bishop is likely to be.—And this leads to the consideration of another passage in the Sermon, which consists of questions not answered :

"Where will you find any authority in God's Word for the distinction drawn in the Roman

Catholic Church between venial and mortal sin ?
Where in God's Word will you find any authority
for purgatory ? where in that word will you find any
authority for the celibacy of the priesthood ? for the
denial of the cup to the laity ? for the doctrine of
transubstantiation ? for the sacrifice of the mass ?
for the adoration of the Virgin ? for the worship of
saints and angels? for all those legends, and miracles,
and lying wonders which are currently believed
among the members of the Roman Catholic Church?"

It would be quite enough to reply to these questions :
Where do you find commandment in the Scriptures for
changing the Sabbath to the Sunday ; for the celebration
of infant baptism ; for Confirmation ; for the reading of
the New Testament,—as the sole rule of the Christian
faith ? It is very remarkable,—at least it should be to
Protestants,—that there is not a text in the Bible, from
one end to the other, for the private interpretation of the
New Testament. St. Paul spoke of the Old Testament
as being able to make St. Timothy " wise unto salvation,"
alluding, of course, to the sufficiency of the Old Testament as a witness to the Messiahship of Christ. And our
Lord said to the Jews : " Search the Scriptures " (that
was, the books of the Old Testament), " for in them ye
think ye have eternal life;" but He immediately proceeded
to upbraid these very readers for being none the wiser for
their reading. There is not a word in the Old Testament, any more than in the New, which justifies the
Protestant theory ; though there is a vast deal which
" plainly contradicts " it. In addition to those many
passages which point to authority, as determining the
doctrines of Christianity, there are those words of St.
Peter which warn the " unstable and the unlearned "
(that is, the immense majority of all readers) against
" wresting " the Scriptures " to their destruction."—But
to proceed with our questions, in retort to the Bishop.
Let us playfully enquire—for we may be playful on this

theme—Where do you find commandment for the marriage
of the clergy, for the servility of the clergy to the State,
for such a "type" as the clergy of the Four Georges, in
short, for a purely secular clergy? Where do you find
commandment for the doctrine of the Real Absence, for
transforming a church into a reading room, for making
the "pure" worship of God as contemptibly human as
Queen Elizabeth's politics or theology? Where do you
find commandment for making a Queen the Head of the
Church, for the appointment of Bishops by a Prime
Minister, or for episcopal jurisdiction through the
Treasury? Where do you find commandment for Penal
Laws against Catholics, for punishing with imprisonment
the not attending "Dearly Beloved Brethren," for hanging
priests by the score for saying Mass, and for hunting
down all Catholics like dogs?* Where do you find
commandment,—though this belongs rather to prophecy,
and we should look for it, say, in Isaiah,—where do you
find the prophecy that, in the sixteenth century, a certain
wicked King should arise, who, wanting to commit
adultery, but being forbidden by the Pope, should
straightway Protestantise the Church? We might
imagine the Protestant Scriptures to contain such a
prophecy as the following: Behold, in the sixteenth
century, the most murderous King shall form an entirely
new Church; assisted by a miserable apostate monk—
whose sole credential for his divine mission shall be found
the fact that he shall seduce a nun from her vows. This

* It is true that, in the short reign of Mary, certain Catholic priests retaliated on Protestants
for the persecution they had endured under Henry. But there is this distinction between persecution by Catholics and persecution by any kind of Protestants: that (1) Catholics were contending
for inalienable rights, held in England for ten centuries; whereas Protestants were torturing and
hanging Catholics for refusing to be robbed by *them.* (2) The infallible might consistently force
truth on the fallible,—that is, with sheer logical consistency; but for a new sect which was con-
fessedly fallible to persecute anybody for anything was equally malignant and ridiculous. (3) All
Christian Governments, as well as all Christian people, held heresy to be the greatest of crimes,
against God as well as against the State; whereas Protestantism had just started the novel
hypothesis that heresy was a simple impossibility. We are not now defending persecution: we are
merely pointing out inconsistencies.—And here we would just notice Mr. Gladstone's last pamphlet, on the subject of the Vatican Decrees; for that pamphlet seems likely to rekindle persecution, by the "No Popery" cry which it inflames. Mr. Gladstone ignores the ostensible fact, that
it is because the State has made encroachments on the Church—greater encroachments than it has
made in past centuries—that therefore the Church is in duty compelled to issue defensive decrees.
When marriage and education are stripped by the State of their essentially religious characteristics; when Modern Thought strives its utmost to uproot all belief, by attacks on the foundations
of Faith; it is the duty of the Pope to warn Catholics *and* Protestants against the snares which
are set for their ruin. Not the Church, but the world, is aggressive; and Mr. Gladstone should be
wiser than to hazard persecution, by totally inverting facts.

murderous King, having formed a new religion, by means
of his headsmen and his jailers, shall hand it on to a
Queen, who, by forty years' cruelty, shall perfe&ct the new
religion.   The people shall be compelled to adopt the new
religion, by fines, imprisonments, and hangings; the most
enduring persecution ever known upon earth being proved
necessary to enforce the Reformation.   This will be that
pure and perfe&ct dispensation which shall supersede (in
Britain) a thousand years of faith, of obedience, of Divine
peace, of Divine unity, of Divine Church.—We do not
find this stated in prophecy; though certainly in Holy
Scripture we do read of "the abomination of desolation,"
which, we presume, refers to the Protestant religion.
And here we may once more ask, is there any prophecy
in the Scriptures, which has the following bearing : that,
for the first fifteen centuries of Christianity, the living
Voice of the Church should teach ; but that about the
year 1450, the invention of printing should supersede
ecclesiastical authority, and letter-press extinguish infallibility ?   Is it mentioned in the Gospels, that though, for
a vast number of centuries, Christians should not be able
to know the truth, because "the circulation of the Bible"
would be impossible, still, the time would come, when,
thanks to John Gutenberg, it would be possible for all
Christians to have a Bible ?   All the Christianity which
was to precede "Art of Printing" was to be "Popish,"
"corrupt," "unscriptural," but when compositors should
arise, and stereotype be invented, then Christianity should
become pure.   This is not stated in the Gospels.
And lastly : Do we read, in any part of the New Testament, that about the sixteenth century—for the first time
in the Church's life—true Christianity should consist in
heresies, in se&cts, in divisions, in schisms ; in self-pleasing,
self-obeying, self-worshipping ; in a luxurious clergy ; in
wedded bishops ; in the soft silken effeminacy of Anglican
palaces, and the easy parsonage houses of married priests ;
in the refusal to obey any authority, save the authority
of one's own private judgment ; in refusing to confess, to

fast, to keep holy-day; in hating the Church, and reviling her Commandments, and preaching twaddle against the "errors of Popery;" in submitting to a Privy Council in matters of ritual, and to oneself only in matters of faith; in prating about the Bible, while interpreting it for oneself, or about the Church, while flatly disobeying it; in worshipping God by a service approved by Parliament, and in swearing to Parliamentary articles; in taking office from a secular Minister, and jurisdiction from a secular First Lord; in obeying Councils just so far as they obey *us*, and in *not* obeying the Vicar of God; in inventing one's own religion, one's own creed, one's own "Bible," and in reducing God to the level of our opinions; in making Christianity the most human of religions, because subject to every man's own will: in short, in making a Christianity of one's own, just as one makes one's own politics or philosophy. We read nothing of this in the Bible. We do read exactly the contrary. We read that heresy is of all sins the greatest—while Protestantism declares it to be " Scriptural;" we read that schism is hateful to God—while Protestantism calls it "religious liberty;" we read that rebellion is worse even than witchcraft—while Protestantism calls it "modern enlightenment;" we read that separatists make "sects of perdition"—whereas Protestantism calls them "Scriptural persons." Thus, we fail to trace the "Scripturalness" of that institution, which is denominated Church of England. To our mind, all the heresies that were ever begotten, all the schisms that were ever created, all the infidelities that were ever conceived, are culminated and embosomed and deified in this last "abomination of desolation." It is the apotheosis of every rebellious spirit, of every heretic, schismatic, and arch-rebel, of every "principle" that has undermined faith—because it is the claim of the *right* of being a heretic. It is the enthronement of the divinity of disobedience. Man may become more degraded in rebellion, but he can never become more absolute.

But to address ourselves to the questions asked by the Bishop.

(1) "Where do you find any authority in God's Word," asks his Lordship with charming simplicity, "for the distinction between venial and mortal sin?" Well, really the question is so idle, that it is difficult to answer it gravely. Does any human being, Christian or non-Christian, class murder with irritability, adultery with effeminacy, theft with over-reaching, or blasphemy with levity? It is certain that the Bishop does not do so. He knows as well as we do that there are sins which "kill the soul," while there are sins of mere weakness or carelessness which one deep sigh may wash out. Children are not hanged for disobeying their parents, nor is hell-fire meant for the imperfect. * Common sense, without any Scripture at all, would tell us that the will, *plus* the nature of the sin, make all the difference in desert. There are scores of passages in the Bible, which speak of sins which quench the grace of God ; and these sins are therefore "mortal," that is deadly.* And there are scores of passages in the Bible which speak of the frailties of our nature, and of God's superabundant clemency in looking lightly upon small (repented) sins. There are sins which "cry from the ground," which, as St. Paul says, "go before men to judgment ;" but there are also sins which are referred to as "infirmities ;" as where St. Paul says, "For we have not a High Priest who cannot have compassion on our infirmities." The word "mortal," like the word "Protestant," is vernacular ; and the word "venial," like the word "Popish," is vernacular. Their senses are obvious to everybody. To carp at words is a weak thing in Protestants, who have invented a whole vocabulary of heresy.

(2) "And where in God's Word," asks the Bishop, will you find any authority for purgatory?" This is another example of that force of "plainness" of Scripture on

---

* The Bishop is supposed to pray, at least three times every week, "From all other *deadly* sins, Good Lord deliver us."

which the Bishop equivocally insists. To a Catholic there are many passages in Scripture, which teach the doctrine of purgatory. First, the doctrine is implied in those very many passages which declare that nothing defiled shall enter Heaven. It is implied in those very many passages which speak of punishment for every committed fault. It is implied in our Lord's descent into Limbo ; at least, so theologians have considered. It is directly taught in the Book of Macabees : " It is a good and wholesome thought to pray for the dead :" and perhaps this is one reason why his Lordship objects to consider the " Apocrypha " inspired. It is directly taught in those words of our Lord : " Verily I say unto thee, thou shalt not come out thence till thou hast paid the uttermost farthing." It is directly taught in those words of St. Paul, " Every man's work shall be manifest ; for the day of the Lord shall declare it, because it shall be revealed in fire ; and the fire shall try every man's work, of what sort it is." The misfortune of Protestants is that they pre-judge the Scriptures ; and having made up their minds that a certain truth is not there, they proceed to deny its existence. It is also their misfortune that they must interpret the Scripture solely by the light of their own minds ; since not only have they no Divine Church to guide them, but each clergyman tells them different things. If they could take the Bible as a whole,—which is solely the habit of Catholics ; and if they had Divine Light,—which is solely the privilege of Catholics ; they would understand many things which, by the light of their own minds, they are quite unable to comprehend. Thus, in regard of purgatory, the light which Catholics have on the subjects of holiness, God's infinite justice and perfection, His vast gifts (in the Church) to a Christian, and the paramount duty of obedience, enable Catholics to judge of truths by many *other* (relative) truths, and to give to each its exact place and force. But poor Protestants, jumbling all truths together, and having no knowledge of God beyond the human interpretation

which each one affixes to favourite texts, are at sea, and
in a maze, on the truths of the Church, as well as at
sea, and in a maze on her authority. How can human
interpretation fix the sense of Divine Words, or mere
man teach God what to believe? It belongs to the
infallible Church to fix the doctrines of the Scriptures,
because God is ever present to guide her. As one
fragment of a broken vessel is but a poor indication of
what that vessel would be, if complete; so the fragments
of truth which Protestants possess are but a poor indication of the whole. The Church is complete; a perfect
Divine vessel; and she judges of the whole, and of parts,
of herself; God showing her herself and Him.

(3) "And where do you find authority," asks the
Bishop, "for all those legends and miracles and lying
wonders,which are currently believed among the members
of the Roman Catholic Church?" By lying wonders the
Bishop means false miracles. And the answer, very
briefly, is this: False miracles are a proof of true.
There are no true miracles in the Church of England;
consequently, there are no false. False "legends"
abound in the Church of England: indeed the whole
system and pretence of Protestantism may be sum-
marized as a bundle of false legends; false legends
corrupting history; false legends as to the practice of
Catholics; false legends as to the teaching of the
Church, and as to the spirit of its acceptance by
Catholics. Be it remembered, in explanation of this
point, that protest implies positive teaching; imitation
the existence of a type. Unless there were a positive,
there would not be a negative. Unless there were an
example, there would not be a copy. These truths may
be illustrated as follows: No one has ever thought of
denying the infallibility of the Archbishop of Canterbury, because that State-official has never thought of
asserting it; but hundreds of silly Catholics have denied
the infallibility of the Pope, because the Church has in
all ages believed it. In regard of true doctrines, true
miracles, true traditions—traditions and legends are

very different things indeed; but we cannot go into that now—the Church has to be perpetually judging. The very *raison d'être* of the Catholic Church, so far as her *magisterium* is concerned, is to distinguish the true from the false; just as the very *raison d'être* of the Church of England is to confuse them both together.

Appropriate to this subject is the whole attitude of heresy towards the divine office of the Church. It is the province of heresy to necessitate dogma, as it is its province to necessitate judgment; and therein we see how the power of God compels even His enemies to serve Him. If there had been no heresy, no spirit of doubt, it is just possible we might have had no creeds. The most splendid definitions have been urged on by hostility to the Written or the Unwritten Word. The dogma of the Immaculate Conception was at least hastened by the unnatural disrespect of Protestants for the Mother of God, and by the concomitantly feeble appreciation which they had of the Divinity of her Son; and the dogma of the Infallibility of the Pope—the most magnificent intellectual certainty with which God has enriched human life—was mainly due to that chaos of folly, which Protestantism calls Modern Thought. Heresy has its mission—unknown to itself—to sharpen the outlines of truth; and though it postpones the Divine operations—as, for example, the conversion of the heathen—it causes truth to shine out as the sun. These remarks on the " magisterium " of the Church, in regard of her judgment on doctrines, apply collaterally to the " magisterium " of the Church, in regard of her judgment on miracles. False miracles imply true; false legends imply true; " lying wonders " imply true; but it is for the Church, not for heretics, to judge them.

(4) As to that question of the Bishop: " Where do you find authority in the Scriptures for the worship of saints and angels ?" suffice it very briefly to remark, that the "Communion of Saints" is an impossibility for heretics, because they are outside the Family of God. The Incarnation not only united God with man; it united

man with God; and the membership of the whole Church, in Heaven, on earth, and in purgatory, is a heart-secret, a heart-truth, of purely Christian belief, but inconsistent with any form of heresy. " I believe in the Communion of Saints " has no meaning whatever for Protestants; any more than " I believe in the Holy Catholic Church." Scripture texts would have no bearing for Protestants, on points which they à priori ignore.*

(5) Again : the Bishop asks : " Where do you find authority for the celibacy of the priesthood ?" Well, St. Paul does not speak so highly of marriage as to lead one to infer that he would select that state for the most exalted type of the Christian. He speaks apologetically of marriage : he does not speak apologetically of priesthood. Of marriage he can only say, " He that is married is divided;" and again, " He that is with a wife is solicitous for the things of the world, how he may please his wife ;" whereas he adds, " He that is without a wife is solicitous for the things that belong to the Lord, how he may please God." He also says, in

---

* Since going to press we have read the report of a sermon, which was preached on Sunday, Nov. 1, from the pulpit of Ripon Cathedral, though not by the Bishop of Ripon. It is probable that more folly, more vanity, have been seldom compressed into one effort. Thus, the preacher objects to the " Ave," or " Hail Mary,"on the ground that it is not a Scriptural composition ; whereas everyone should know that the first half is composed of the *ipsissima verba* of Scripture, while the second half is a prayer for intercession. The Archangel Gabriel must have been a heretic, and St. Elizabeth an "unscriptural " person, if the " Ave " is not what it should be. The preacher, too, omits the principal words of the prayer, " Blessed is the fruit of thy womb, Jesus," whether purposely or accidentally we know not. Then, again, he quotes the words of the " Confiteor," which every Catholic says when confessing, as an example of " blasphemous " prayer ; forgetting that at the Day of Judgment—which good confessions anticipate—all sins of all men will be openly confessed before all saints and angels of God. If it is blasphemy now to humble ourselves before Heaven, it will be quite as much blasphemy then. But the preacher thinks nothing of saints, unless *he* has condescended to canonize them. We have seen that, in his opinion, the Archangel Gabriel was a heretic, and St. Elizabeth an unscriptural person; similarly he informs us that " St. Gervase, St. Silvester, St. Fabian, St. Anastasia," were very sorry saints." This is really exquisite as a specimen of presumption—of that complacency which is ready to judge everybody, from the Popes down to cloistered ascetics. He confuses mediators and intercessors, because he finds this convenient ; and he says St. John would have done homage to an angel, for which the angel rebuked him ; whereas he should know that St. John mistook the angel for our Lord, and would have rendered not homage but adoration. Homage may be rendered to anyone, so may worship in the natural sense; but adoration can be rendered only to God—a distinction which Catholics understand. We were quite prepared for what follows ; for " the childish perverseness of Romanists," for " Rome being deaf to all argument," (that is, to Protestant preachers' arguments) for the Church being " the mother of harlots," " Satan's masterpiece," " the mystery of iniquity." This is one fruit of the preacher's " open Bible " which he considers " the glory of his Church !" This is the language which he applies to that religion, which was professed by his forefathers, without the slightest intermission— as the Anglican Homilies assert—" for eight hundred years and more;" for which in our own country Sir Thomas More died, and which was the intellectual joy of a Bossuet and a Fénelon, of St. Bernard and of St. Thomas Aquinas. He forgets that, by such language, he accuses the Son of God of being incompetent to fulfil His own promises, while he accuses the Holy Ghost of teaching the whole Church l s, instead of teaching her " all truth." St. Jude has some words about ignorance and blasphemy, which we commend to the attention of this gentleman : " Hi autem quæcumque quidem ignorant, blasphemant ; quæcumque autem naturaliter, tamquam muta animalia, norunt, in his corrumpuntur."

speaking even of the laity, " It is good for a man not to touch a woman." While of a Bishop he says, " A Bishop should be the husband of one wife ;" that is, a Bishop should *have* been married but once ; for since he dissuaded even the devout laity from marrying,—that is, those of the laity who aimed at perfection,—it is impossible that he should have advised Bishops to enter a state, which he himself pronounced apologetic. He must have meant, then, that a twice married person was too obviously secular and world-bound to be accepted as a candidate for the office. And we must rememember, too, that in St. Paul's days, men were converted to Christianity when they had attained the full maturity of years ; so that what is a question of " discipline " in these days was one of fitness or expediency in those. Be this as it may, we are at liberty to infer that, if St. Paul lived in these days, he would not deliberately make choice of that state which he regarded as imperfect. We cannot conceive of St. Paul, or of St. John, starting on what we now call a wedding tour, acclaimed by bridesmaids, or toasted by groomsmen, or enraptured by the bride's " latest fashions." There are certain incongruities at which the human mind revolts ; and a married apostle is one of them. The Church of England clergy, we know, are not apostles ; they are laymen with the prefix of Reverend,—or Right Reverend, as the Prime Minister may think best. Still, even they ought to be able to comprehend that a " successor of the Apostles " making love to his congregation is a very unseemly sight indeed. A popular preacher may be a congruous idea, in a three volume novel meant for Protestants ; but a preacher whose popularity has nuptial contingents is hardly an apostolic type. It is perfectly proper, we know, that the Protestant clergy should marry—because they are only Protestant clergy. They are not priests in any sense of the word. They have no orders, jurisdiction, nor faculty ; and they minister only to opinion. They have no sacrifice to offer, no confessions to hear, no

Mysteries to handle or proclaim. Theirs is a human religion ; and they, like their religion, are but human. It was not to them that our Lord addressed the words, " He that can receive it, let him receive it." The case is the reverse with true priests. The Adorable Sacrifice is their daily contemplation ; the Sacrament of Penance half their life. They are set apart for supernatural functions, and their whole spirit is far above the world. They are elected of God to be exemplars ; as well as to teach certain truth. Theirs is a life which has little in common with the average aspirations of the laity ; and if anything could add to the dignity of their office, it would be the excellence with which they fulfil it. These men are what they seem to be ; true types of true priests ; asking nothing of their penitents which *they* do not perform ; teaching by example quite as much as by precept ;—a holy and separate class. But the Protestant clergy are mere men of the world ; highly moral, respectable, proper ; but with no shadow of pretence to a supernatural character in their lives any more than in their teaching. Marriage is their first grand idea, and private opinion their second. " Marriage," said Erasmus, " is the only paradise left for a reformed or Protestant Christian;" and certainly—with the exception of hatred for " Popery "—it is the only dogma on which they are agreed. Curates are divided between rapturous sermons or what they are pleased to call " faith," and equally rapturous expatiations on the charms of some member of their flock ; and though all this is very natural and proper in *them*, it would be simply inconceivable in true priests. That spectacle which makes Catholics smile—the spectacle of a wedded ecclesiastic—reaches its apex of fantastic suggestiveness, when a Dean or a Bishop is the example ; and nothing but good breeding prevents Catholics from laughing, when they come across these highly mundane apostles. Even the Russians will not hear of a priest getting married *after* he has taken the first orders : semi-barbarous as they are, that is too much for them : but, then, we must remember that the Russians have true orders.—And this leads to the consideration of the next question of the Bishop : What proof is there of the Doctrine of Transubstantiation.

(6) It is not likely that a "priesthood" which makes marriage its first element would have the faculty of diving deeply into Scripture. Scripture truths are hid, since they are revealed by the Holy Spirit, and the Holy Spirit alone can interpret them. Consequently a class which is uxorious and worldly, differing from lay heretics in nothing but name, and in a slight change of dress and demeanour, could not be expected to have supernatural insight into the truths which lie hid in the Gospel. Even Catholic priests do not presume to fix doctrines until God has taught the Church through His Vicar ; yet the meanest Catholic layman is much more of a priest than all the Anglican Bishops put together. And here let it be remarked, for it is most important to note it, that in every case where true orders are pre-served, as for example in the Schismatical Greek Church, there is preserved also the true Doctrine of the Blessed Sacrament; so that sacrilege has been rendered unlikely. But in the case of English Protestants, who have lost the succession, there was no necessity to preserve the true doctrine, which could have led but to impious counterfeit. Consequently, "Dearly Beloved Brethren," and a commemorative communion, have taken the place of the Real Presence with Protestants; while the Greeks have preserved the true doctrine of the Blessed Sacra-ment, concurrently with Apostolic order.

And certainly it may be permitted to observe at this point, that Protestants of the school of the Bishop of Ripon have much more consistency on their side than the so-called Anglo-Catholic clergy; for to hold that sacrifice, consecration, or even *one* gift of priesthood, is retained by the Anglican clergy is to charge three cen-turies of Protestants with the blackest infidelity, or with supreme unconsciousness of their gifts. If Protestants had the true priesthood, it would be impossible

to contemplate the sacrilege of millions of their
"Communions." Happily, everybody knows that they
have not.

Now the Bishop puts three questions close together;
and it will be better that we answer them as one. He
wants to know what authority there is in the Scriptures
for (1) "Transubstantiation," for (2) "Sacrifice," for
(3) "the denial of the cup to the laity." The answer
to any one is the answer to all three; because if we
grant the authority of the Church, in determining the
teaching of Scripture, it is certain that the Church
cannot lead us astray on one point any more than on
another. But there is an answer which is also com-
prehensive, and satisfactory to the rational thinker. *If*
Transubstantiation be true—and we will here first argue
on hypothesis—it must follow, first, that we should offer
Christ in sacrifice, and, secondly, that we *need not*
receive the Chalice. Of the first, let us say that, to
possess Christ on our altars, and not to offer Him to
the Father, would be as impossible as not to plead
Christ in prayer when we address the Father in Heaven.
And, of the second, it is obvious that, if the Host be
Very God, then is God present in each species of the
Sacrament, that is, He is present in both. And here
we must observe that there is something quite childish,
something utterly inconsistent and irrational, in blaming
the Church for depreciating the Sacrament, while at
the same time blaming her for exalting it! If the
Catholic Church teach Transubstantiation, she must
teach that the Real Presence is complete in the Host,
and also in each drop in the Chalice. There is no
dividing Christ. As it was customary in the Early
Church to give the Chalice to the very young, and also
to the infirm or the sick, because the Chalice, like the
Host, is God; so is it reasonable to give the Host by
itself, because the Host, without the Chalice, is God.
The motive of the Church in withholding the Cup is not
one that we need now discuss. Probably reverence had
a good deal to do with it, since the giving the Chalice

led to accidents ; and there was also the desire to protest against heresy—the heresy which Protestants proclaim. But, whatever the motives, we say that for Protestants, who degrade the true doctrine of the Real Presence, to upbraid the Church for maintaining it, is irrational, and even wantonly absurd, and exposes them to be answered with ridicule.

As regards the testimony of Scripture on this point, we think it is perfectly sufficient. We do not presume to judge the Scriptures for ourselves ; since the variety of gifts, and the vastness of requirements, which are necessary for even its natural interpretation, lie outside the possession of most men ; but, speaking primâ facie, we should conclude that our Lord's words would justify the practice of the Church. The Council of Trent well remarks : " He who said, ' Except ye eat, &c.,' said also, ' He that eateth of this bread shall live for ever ;' and He who said, ' He that eateth My flesh and drinketh My blood hath eternal life,' said at the same time, ' The bread which I will give is My flesh for the life of the world.'" Then again, when our Lord said, " This do," we cannot for a moment conclude that He meant *all* men to do what He then did ; for if this were so, it might belong to all men and to all women to consecrate as well as to partake. Nor from the words, " Drink ye all of it," can we fairly infer that all mankind were included in the commandment ; for the " all " relates evidently to the Apostles, and not to the Chalice of the Precious Blood. The word " do " is an ordinary expression, both with sacred and secular writers, for " offer sacrifice." In the Septuagint it is so used many times ; it is so applied to the paschal sacrifice ; and that this was its meaning, in the institution of the Holy Sacrifice, the Church has taught us to believe. Where difficulties of scholarship, of complex erudition, cross the path of the student of the Scriptures, it is wiser to trust to the Spirit of God, than to man's judgment, for the right interpretation ; and we Catholics are happy in

not having to risk our souls on the " private interpretation of the Scriptures." But with regard to Transubstantiation—which the Bishop of Ripon thinks is not
taught in any part of the New Testament—we Catholics
are of opinion that it is simply impossible for language
to teach Transubstantiation more "plainly." Of course,
the " plainness " of Scripture, on this point as on every
other, is purely a matter of appreciation; for just as
Catholics marvel at the blindness of Protestants, in not
reading the Pope's primacy in the Gospels; in not
detecting the Divine office of the priesthood; in not
seeing the immaculateness of Mary, and her maternity
to the whole Christian Church, from the very first word
of the Gospels to the very last; in not tracing the
characteristics of the Visible Church and the capitalness
of the crime of all heresy; in not seeing how they are
themselves condemned in the Bible—in the Old Testament as well as in the New—for that very offence which
is singled out for punishment of an exceptional and
terrible kind; so do Catholics marvel that the doctrine
of Transubstantiation is hid from even their natural
eyes. But then we remember that there is no heresy
of Protestantism, no outrageous parody of the Church,
which is not " proved most plainly from the Scriptures,"
to the satisfaction and consolation of the heretic. Protestants forget—to quote the Archbishop of Westminster—that " Holy Scripture is Holy Scripture only
in the right sense of Holy Scripture;" and they fancy
that anything is Holy Scripture which *they* are pleased
to approve. Thus, Bishop Colenso quotes eleven texts
of Scripture against offering prayer to our Blessed Lord ;
and the extremest advocates of " Romanizing " doctrine,
like the extremest advocates of rabid Dissent, quote
texts by the score for their views ; and very good texts
they (verbally) are. Exeter Hall and the Privy Council,
Convocation and Mr. Spurgeon, Brother Ignatius and
Mr. Jowett, Mr. Bennett and Dean Stanley, are all
ready with an avalanche of texts, to bear down their
opponents in theology. The " plainness " of Scripture !

Why, if the "plainness" of Scripture mean anything at all, in the Church of England sense of the word, it can only mean that it does not matter one straw what a man believes about anything.—But to return to our immediate theme : what proof is there in the Bible of Transubstantiation? "Amen, Amen, I say to you, except ye eat the flesh of the Son of Man, and drink His blood, ye shall not have life in you : He that eateth My flesh and drinketh My blood hath everlasting life, and I will raise him up at the last day : for My flesh is meat indeed, and My blood is drink indeed : " this is language which leaves us no doubt, in regard of the truth of our belief. When the Jews took exception to the doctrine of Transubstantiation, our Lord merely suffered them to go away; confirming, however, His already spoken words by an equally distinct asseveration. Again, "Drink ye all of this, for this is My blood of the New Testament, which shall be shed for you and for many for the remission of sins," appears to Catholics to mean Transubstantiation. "He that eateth My flesh and drinketh My blood dwelleth in Me, and I in him ;" as also, "He that eateth of this bread shall live for ever," are expressions which, to us, bear no other interpretation than such as the Church puts upon them. There are other passages of similar "plainness," not less strong, not less patent, than the consecrating words, "This is My body." And St. Paul uses language of much the same force, over and over again, in his Epistles. "Therefore whosoever shall eat of this bread, or drink of the Cup of the Lord unworthily, shall be guilty of the body and blood of the Lord." The Chalice of Benediction which we bless, is it not the Communion of the Blood of Christ ; and the bread which we break, is it not the partaking of the Body of the Lord ?" He speaks, too, of "not discerning the Lord's body," and he says, "We are members of His body, of His flesh, and of His bones," with other passages of similar import. So that anyone who can say that there is *no* testimony in Scripture for the Catholic doctrine of the

Blessed Sacrament, says what—to use the Bishop's language—"plainly contradicts God's Word." And so, too, of the doctrine of Sacrifice. We have spoken of the probable sense of that passage, "This *do*, in remembrance of Me;" and since the Church takes these words in a sacrificial sense, as well as in a commemorative and communicative, we are wise in following her teaching. We must remember that, in the institution of the Blessed Sacrament, the words, not the actions, are given; what our Lord may have *done* being left mainly untold; what He *said* being expressly written down. This is vastly significant and important. It was not the intention of the Evangelists to forestall the future teaching of the Church; to treat compendiously and in detail of all ritual; it was their intention to summarize the history of Redemption, and such doctrines as were to be primarily of faith. Just as in regard of the Sabbath, there is no written commandment for the change; so, in regard of many doctrines, much is left to apostolical tradition. To the Catholic, the Blessed Sacrament being the life of the Church,—the Holy Sacrifice, the Adorable Presence being her joys,—any doubt thrown on the doctrine of Transubstantiation sounds like hideous ingratitude and impiety. To the Protestant, whose Churches are but rooms for human voices, arenas for human controversy, human guess, the Blessed Sacrament is but an occasional commemoration, without even definite belief. No wonder that, possessing only such fragments of Christianity as they have borrowed from the teaching of the Church, but borrowed mainly to corrupt, they are unable to grasp that mighty Divine whole, which is the most perfect work of God upon earth. They read their Bibles; and when, in the prophecy of Malachias, they find these words, "For, from the rising of the sun, even to the going down, My Name is great among the Gentiles; and in every place there is Sacrifice, and there is offered to My Name a clean oblation," they fail to see what the Church sees— the prophecy of the Sacrifice of the Mass. They read of Melchisedech, as offering a sacrifice, a sacrifice like the Christian of bread and wine ; and they read, too, that Christ was " a priest for ever according to the order of Melchisedech ;" but they fail to see the truth which the Church sees, that this figure has reference to the Mass. They read those words of St. Paul, " We have an altar ;" but they admit not the Christian altar. Where is the use of a Bible, which for *them* has no definite teaching ? The truth is, the Bible is a supernatural book, and is not to be naturally apprehended. For this reason it is that, in England, we have sects, which are almost beyond the reach of our counting ; divisions *in* the Church of England which baffle computation, and " faiths " which defy all analysis. Protestantism is another name for Chaos ; and Protestants knowing this are agreed on one point—that they will unite in protesting against the Church. Unity of belief being impossible for Protestants, they compound by unity of protest.

(7) And this brings us to the consideration of another statement of the Bishop, which we will quote in his Lordship's own words :

" I emphatically deny the boasted unity of the Church of Rome. Who has read ecclesiastical history, but must be aware of the almost numberless contentions amongst Roman Catholics ? Who has not heard of rival Popes and rival Councils ? One Pope anathematizing what another Pope held true, and so with Councils. There is uniformity, I admit, outward superficial uniformity, and outward allegiance to one visible head, who falsely calls himself the vicar or vicegerent of Christ on earth, but there is not unity ; on the other hand, I maintain that amongst the overwhelming majority of Protestants there is this deep, essential, true unity, which Rome has never been able to obtain, and which exists, notwithstanding the absence of external uniformity. The truth is, you may have unity without uniformity, and you may have visible uniformity without unity, and which is to be valued most ?"

When the Bishop talks about Catholic unity, he is unfortunately talking about a subject of which he knows absolutely nothing. That unity results, first, from the gift of faith ; a gift which, in its plentitude, is only possible to Catholics, who alone possess all Christian truth. It results, secondly, from the possession of a definite creed, taught by infallible authority ; so that a Catholic both knows what he has to believe, and believes by the Divine gift of faith. Thirdly, there is just as much liberty of opinion, on matters that are *not* " de fide," among Catholics as there is among Protestants ; and it is one of the most striking proofs of the Divinity of the Church, that, while she can leave all her members to run wild in opinions, she can bind them in matters of faith. The contentions of theologians, before a truth is defined, prove the perfect liberty of all Catholics in opinions ; just as the submission of opponents to a truth which is defined proves the perfect integrity of their faith. This double truth was shown during the last Council ; when the few who had opposed the definition of "Infallibility"—opposed it sincerely and dutifully—submitted as ardently as they had opposed. Here is the difference between the Catholic and the heretic. The heretic cares for nothing but his own opinions ; and neither Pope nor Council, inspired writer nor Saint, can turn him from his stubborn resolve. But a Catholic knows that he may contend about opinions, but must not contend against dogma; nor is there anything more edifying in the history of the Church than the submission of opponents to decree. When the Bishop of Ripon talks of "rival Popes and rival Councils," "one Pope anathematizing what another Pope holds true, and so with Councils," he is unconsciously touching on one of the very strongest proofs of the personal infallibility of the Popes. The Bishop's statement is of course incorrect : no Pope has ever anathematized what another Pope taught, nor has any *true* Council falsified a *true*. But the events to which he incorrectly alludes are marvellous proofs of the Church's belief in the personal infallibility of the Pope. Thus, in the case of Pope Honorius, we have the Council which condemned him,—not for "heresy," but, as Dr. Döllinger says, for "inactivity" —declaring that "*all* the Apostolic Pontiffs had confirmed the brethren in the faith," and that "the Roman Church had *never* turned aside from the path of truth to any error whatsoever," nor "had it *ever* been obscured by heresy, nor defiled by error." The language of the Council seems studiedly emphatic in regard of the infallibility of Popes; as though the Council foresaw—what indeed has been the case—that heretics would misinterpret its judgment. The same teaching is observed, when the contentions of false Popes (set up by princely ambition) had been made to give place to obedience. The Council of Constance, which was mainly called to decide between the true Pope and shameless pretenders, taught the personal infallibility of the Sovereign Pontiff in language which was severely distinct : "It is impossible that such a See (the Roman) should determine, and hold, for the Catholic faith that which is not the true faith." And Martin V., who was declared the true Pope, issued a decree to the Council in session : "It is not lawful for any person to appeal from the Sovereign Pontiff, who is the Supreme Judge, and the Vicar of Christ on earth; or by subterfuge to elude his judgment in matters of faith." And this decree was acclaimed by the Council, not one of the Bishops dissenting. Thus the very scandals of the ambitious have been converted by God into occasions for splendid out-speaking. While in regard of false Councils, the explanation is this : that no decree of any Council could be of value in the Church, unless ratified by the Sovereign Pontiff; so that we have more than one example, in the history of the Church, of the Pope setting aside the decisions of Councils—Councils not Œcumenical but local—when such decisions were not approved by himself. As Dr. Döllinger tells us, in his "History of the Church," the sole authority for determining the validity of any Council, the validity of its session, of its decrees, was God's Vicar, the Bishop of

Rome ; and Dr. Döllinger quotes examples (which fill many pages) of this radical principle in the Church. " That the decrees of Synods regarding faith obtained their full force and authority, *only* by being received and confirmed by the Pope, was publicly acknowledged in the fourth century." So says Dr. Döllinger in his " History." While in regard of the infallibility of the Pope, the same author is at pains to declare : " It was a thing unheard of that the Head of the Church should be placed in judgment before his own subjects. . . . He who was not in communion with the Bishop of Rome was not truly in the Catholic Church. . . . It was acknowledged to be the prerogative of the first See in the Christian world, that the Bishop of Rome could be judged by no man." Such was the language of Dr. Döllinger, before he fell away from the faith. Indeed, the whole history of the dogmas of the Church is the history of the decisions of Popes. The Vicar of God, who, as Dr. Döllinger tells us, was called in the very first ages, " the Father of Fathers, the Shepherd and Guardian of the flock of Christ, the Chief of all Bishops, the Guardian of the Vineyard of Christ," was the sole arbiter of Councils as of individuals, the supreme authority over the whole living Church. This is the explanation of that repudiation of certain Councils, to which the Bishop of Ripon alludes. We can excuse the Bishop for mis-reading Church history, since his sources are Protestant, and therefore prejudiced;*

---

* The private interpretation of history is as much a weakness of Protestants as the private interpretation of Scripture. A few Sundays ago, in the Cathedral of Ripon, some remarks were made on Galileo, which showed that the preacher interpreted history as freely as he interpreted the Bible. Granted that it is most difficult to know the particulars of events which occurred 250 years ago, still, there are broad facts which any one may learn, any one who will take the trouble to do so. Let us trace the broad facts as to Galileo.

(1) It is to Rome that we are mainly indebted for what is called the Copernican theory. It was a Roman Cardinal, Nicolas of Susa, who is believed to have first publicly broached it, and who was rewarded for his labours by the Pope. Forty years later came Copernicus, who delivered lectures in Rome by command of Pope Leo X., held a conspicuous professorial chair, and published his treatise on the heliocentric theory by the command of, and by the aid of, Paul III. This work went forth to the world, bearing the written sanction of the Pope. Galileo was a Tuscan. In his day the Copernican theory was taught in the lectures of the Roman College, and also in the Sapienza, the Pope's own University. But the ignorant populace—not the Pope, nor the Cardinals, nor the wise men in the Church—took scandal at a theory which apparently contradicted certain very plain statements of Scripture. And now Galileo made his ruinous mistake. Copernicus had been content to confine himself to science ; but Galileo must prove his theory from Scripture. He was warned off such ground by authority. A friend of Pope Urban VIII. wrote—by command of that Pontiff—to entreat Galileo to desist : " You ought not to travel out of the limits of physics and mathematics ; you should confine yourself to such reasoning as Ptolemy and Copernicus used : theologians maintain that the interpretation of Scripture is their own particular care." But Galileo would *force* the Inquisition to pronounce judgment on the Scripturalness of his theory. He was again entreated to desist, in the

and we can excuse him for being perfectly incompetent to understand the unity of the Church, because he is outside it, and will, we fear, remain so ; but when he talks of "the deep, essential, true unity of Protestants,"— are we to assume that he jests ? In Ripon alone he will find more religions than he will find in all China or Persia. And the very incapacity of the Bishop to detect this disunion—if indeed we must take his words in earnest—proves his incompetency to teach. It proves even that he is not acquainted with the radical distinction between a Catholic and any kind of heretic. A heretic is a person who chooses for himself, instead of obeying the Church ; and whether he chooses one thing or another makes no difference whatever in the fact of his

---

most friendly, even affectionate terms. He promised to leave Scripture alone. He subsequently broke that promise, in the most impetuous, even insolent manner. Meanwhile, Pope Urban VIII. was elevating to the very highest positions those who held the Copernican theory ; and, among them, Galileo himself, who received a pension as a reward for his labours.

(2) It was solely out of reverence to the Holy Scriptures, and to avoid giving scandal to the weak, that Galileo was punished at all ; and were it not that the hatred of Popery is stronger than the love of the Bible in the hearts of the majority of Protestants, they would applaud the Church for her conduct. To show that the Church was not singular, in wishing to ward off this scandal, it may be mentioned that when Kepler, a German Protestant, wrote a book in 1596 to vindicate the Copernican system, and submitted it to the Protestant Academical Senate of Tubingen, it was pronounced to be "damnable heresy ;" and he was driven into a Catholic country to take refuge from Protestant wrath. We must remember, too, in palliation of this course, that even down to the days of Sir Isaac Newton the Copernican system was not proved ; and therefore the sense of Scripture might well be held in abeyance in regard of a purely astronomical point. True or not true, the avoidance of scandal to even one soul in the Christian Church was of far more importance in the eyes of good men than all astronomical points put together.

(3(The Pope did not issue a "dogma" on the subject ; but the Council of the Inquisition passed a disciplinary judgment, to counteract the irreverence of Galileo. To understand this it must be known that (1) the Pope is not infallible on astronomy, and therefore could not teach *ex cathedrâ* upon it. Neither in regard of an astronomical theory, nor of the bearing of Scripture upon it, could the Pope affect to teach dogmatically. The Pope is infallible on faith and morals, but fallible on everything else : so that he could not teach infallibly on a point which lay outside his judicial inerrancy. (2) No judgment was given on the true sense of Scripture ; only a condemnation of Galileo's special errors ; and what those special errors were, only they can understand who have read through the whole of his writings. And how many moderns have done this? Again, (3) the word "heresy," applied to these writings, did not mean theological heresy. The Inquisition being first formed to judge of heresy in doctrine, the word heresy was necessarily employed, so as to render a process legal, and to enable the "qualifiers" to proceed. This word was used, up to the time of the Reformation, to convey any offence against the Church ; as where Martin Luther, when speaking of some prefect who did not pay tribute to the Pope, said, "Such impertinence must always in the Pope's spiritual law be called heresy." That Galileo did not think himself condemned, in even so much as the "scientific" sense, is apparent from his letter to a friend : "The result has not been favourable to my enemies ; because the doctrine of Copernicus has not been declared heretical, but only as not consonant with Holy Scripture ;" that is, with the "primâ facie" signification of Scripture. The Pope also wrote : "The Copernican system is not condemned, nor is it to be considered heretical, but only as rash." And, forthwith, one of the Cardinals, by command of the Pope, issued a new edition of Galileo's writings ; eliminating the passages on the Scriptures, and reducing the theory to hypothesis.

(4) As to the punishment of Galileo, so absurdly exaggerated by adversaries, he passed a week in the Dominican Convent of Minerva in Rome, and four months in the palace of the Tuscan Ambassador, his own particular friend. "I have for a prison," he wrote, in a letter which is extant, "the delightful Palace of Trinita di Monte." Subsequently, he wrote, "Afterwards they sent me to my best friend, the Archbishop of Siehna, and I have always enjoyed the most delightful tranquility." Later he went to his own villa. in Florence, where he died in peace with the Church —So that the clemency of the Church in the punishment of a rebel, even of one who had caused great scandal, is not less shown in this story of Galileo, than is her nurture of science—apart from theology—and her reverence in thet reatment of Scripture.

being a heretic. If a man believe the truth on nineteen doctrines of Christianity, but disobey the Church on the twentieth, he is just as much a heretic as though he started a new religion, or preached in a Protestant Cathedral. Obedience to the Church is the sole test of orthodoxy ; disobedience is the act of heresy ; for in the mere fact that a man pleases himself in preference to obeying the Church, he is cut off from Catholic unity, and is sunk in mortal sin. He may preach about the " wonderful grace of our Lord Jesus Christ, and the quickening, enlightening influence of the Holy Spirit," as most heretics have done, from Valentinus to Spurgeon—between the Councils of Jerusalem and the Vatican ; but as St. Polycarp said to Marcion, who claimed fellowship with him, " I know thee for the first-born of hell." The greater the heretic, the greater his profession of " belief in the merits of Christ ;" for he must hide his disobedience in gushing sentiment, and in professing what none can deny. It is, indeed, one of the most comic features of heresy, that it talks as though heresy had just discovered Christ, and the Church knew nothing about Him ! It is commonly supposed, by those who have the truth, that the saints and the martyrs of the Catholic Church — that is, eighteen centuries of saints and of martyrs—have known some little about "the merits of Christ," and have reduced that knowledge to practice. St. Ignatius and St. Ambrose, St. Cyril and St. Chrysostom, St. Basil and St. Gregory the Great, St. Bernard, St. Bonaventure, and St. Thomas of Canterbury, who were " Roman Catholics " to the very depths of their souls, were men who could have taught Protestants a knowledge of Christ which at present appears to them unattainable. With *them* the knowledge of Christ was of faith ; with Protestants it is only of sentiment.* And any one of

* The points of contact between faith and sentiment are scarcely discernible by Protestants, though they are clear as the sun to Catholics. Let us take a familiar example. In a Catholic church there is one sovereign idea, which overrules every relative or auxiliary, namely, the Presence of God. Whether a church be handsome or ugly, the decorations exquisite or absurd, the music in good taste or in bad, the Catholic knows only one Presence—God. This is faith *versus* sentiment. Whereas in a Protestant church, God being not present,—the Blessed Sacrament being practically banished,—the furniture, the music, the *mise en scene* (and, above all, the popular

these saints, and scores of others who were like them, would have told the Bishop of Ripon to make haste to confess, to submit, and to be received into the Church. They would have told him—had they lived in our own day—that he was not even a sub-deacon ; and that, just as likely as not, he was unbaptized—through the shameful carelessness in the administration of that Sacrament, which has been characteristic of the Anglican Church. While, in the words of our Lord, they would have warned every Catholic, " He that will not hear the Church, let him be to thee as a heathen and a publican." They would have told the Bishop of Ripon that " St. Peter's Chair is the root and womb of the Church," and that " he who abandons the Chair of Peter cannot flatter himself that he is in the Church " (St. Cyprian) ; that " this is the Rock which hell's proud gates shall never conquer ;" that " in the Chair of Peter Christ hath placed the doctrines of truth.   . . Those severed from the Communion of the Catholic Church, that is, not *agreeing* in all things with the Apostolic See, shall not have their names recited in the sacred Mysteries " (St. Augustine) ; that " whosoever in any way separate themselves from the unity of his faith—the Pope's—or his society, such are not able to be absolved from the bonds of their sins, nor to enter the threshold of the Heavenly Kingdom " (Venerable Bede) ; that he who renders not reverently to him," the Pope, " due obe- dience, involves himself, as being severed from the Head, in the schism of the Acephali " (St. Isidore) ;

preacher) usurp the place of the Most Holy. This is sentiment *versus* faith. It is only of late years that that singular fabric, denominated Protestant Church, has assumed æsthetic charac- teristics. Up to thirty years ago, a Protestant church was a room ; containing three big boxes, each rising above the other, scores of hideous cowpens called pews, a communion table which was specially constructed to protest against the presence of God, and a lion and a unicorn in playful combination between two tablets of Judaic commandments. The Protestant, when he entered his church, knew that God was not there ; so he put his face into his hat, and his feet on a hassock, with ostentatious declaration of Real Absence. But in a Catholic church, though the sentiment may be bad, the taste really shocking to refinement, the music unfitted for a church, and the auxiliaries tawdry or poor, still *there* is the Real Presence, and there is the Divine Sacrifice, with true priesthood, true function, true everything. The Catholic can smile at shortcomings in art, because he has the certainties of faith. Indeed, a Catholic Church is earth's Heaven—to the intellect, though not to the senses. Just as in Heaven the Lord Jesus Christ is offering Himself perpetually to the Father, so on earth, from the altars of God, He is perpetually doing the same. The Divine Sacrifice is the same sacrifice, on earth, which is offered without interval in Heaven; the Divine Presence is the same Presence, on our altars, which is "seated at the right hand of God." All that nonsense which is talked from some pulpits, about "the Mass making void Christ's Sacrifice," shows that the preachers are as ignorant of the worship of Heaven as they are of true worship on earth.

that "all dangers and scandals emerging in the Kingdom of God, especially those which concern faith, must be referred to *your*—the Pope's—apostolate ; for it is fitting that the injuries done to faith should be repaired there where faith cannot fail " (St. Bernard) ; that "the Pope cannot err. . . . Before him who holds the place of Christ every knee must bend on earth, as before Christ in Heaven " (St. Bonaventure) ; with whole volumes of similar teaching, in all ages, all countries, of the Church. And if the Bishop of Ripon could get himself for one moment to listen to the teaching of the Church, he would learn why it is that heresy is a great crime, nay, greater than all crimes put together. Whereas most other sins that a man can commit are committed against the Commandments of God, the sin of heresy is that exceptional sin which is committed against the Person of God; it is the direct attack on His Essence, His Being ; it is a personal onslaught on God. Truth being Divine, an attack on any *one* Divine truth is an attack on God's unity, Himself. To hear Protestants talk, you would imagine that the truth was the exclusive private property of each of them ; that God had nothing to do with it, save so far as they would allow Him, and would kindly consent to instruct Him. They are "liberal" with God's truth ; which is a peculiar form of liberality—to be liberal with what does not belong to them. And they preach about " freedom in religious opinions ;" as if freedom consisted in being in bondage to oneself, or to ten thousand contradictory teachers. The only Christians in the world who are " free," who enjoy unrestricted religious liberty, are the members of the Catholic Church ; because God being their teacher, they cannot believe lies, and are therefore free from the bondage of error. All Protestants are in bondage either to their private opinions—which are necessarily absurd because human—or to some Bishop or clergyman of their sect ; and they are bound hand and foot by fantastic traditions, latest " views," or the teaching of their

parents or friends. As an American writer observes:
"There is no bondage so gross as that of Protestants
to their preachers, unless it be that of Pagans to their
idols." And as a natural result of this bondage—either
to themselves or to their preachers—they are unable to
distinguish between the "act" of heresy, and the particular heresies they adopt. This is the case with
the Bishop. He talks about the unity of Protestants;
thus showing that, in the first place, he has lost sight
of the fact that there is such a sin as heresy; and that,
as a consequence, he is profoundly indifferent to each
and to all kinds of that sin. His position obliges these
two evils. To be in communion with clergymen who
flatly contradict him on what *they* deem "essentials in
belief" is to maintain that it is a matter of perfect in-
difference whether the clergy teach one thing or another.
To say that there is no testimony in Scripture for the
Mass, while scores of English clergy "say Mass," (of
course they do not say it, but they pretend to,) is to
proclaim that it does not matter whether Mass is
idolatry, or the Adorable Sacrifice of the altar. These
High Churchmen have the same right to their private
Christianities as any Bishop or Archbishop of their
Church; they are clergy, are of the very same communion; they live in the same disobedience to Rome,
as to their own superiors on their right hand or their
left: what is to prevent *them* from being right, or the
Bishop of Ripon from being wrong; and what authority
is to judge between them? There is none. Some years
ago Mr. Bennett, of Frome, was asked by the Archbishop of Armagh, "Do you consider yourself a sacrificing priest?" He replied, "Yes." When further
pressed by these words, "In fact, *sacerdos*, a sacrificing
priest?" he answered, "Certainly." Yet Mr. Bennett
remains in cheerful communion with scores of clergymen like the Bishop of Ripon, who flatly deny the
"*sacerdos*." So, Archdeacon Denison was condemned
by the Archbishop of Canterbury—unjustly and absurdly
we admit—and deprived of his Church preferments;

that is, he would have been deprived, but for an appeal to the Privy Council ; an appeal which he had himself protested against in the case of the Gorham controversy. The fact is that an Anglican clergyman will remain in communion with anybody ; and very logically too ; for he knows that there is no real authority in his Church, save only private opinion. Both the High Church party—which judges the Early Church, the Popes, the Councils, the Doctors, the Saints, Anglican Bishops, *as well as* the teaching of the Scriptures ; and the Low Church party—which limits its sovereignty to the infallible (private) interpretation of the Scriptures ; would remain in communion with any arch-priest of heresy, because they know that their Church is but a Club. The "Old Catholics" have been recently invited to join that Club ; or rather they have half invited themselves ; for every one knows that to rebel against the Pope is the first condition for admission. The "Old Catholics" had opportunity allowed them for repentance ; the Pope behaved to them leniently ; but at last they were cut off from the Church ; cast headlong into the abyss of heresy ; left friendless, alone, in the world. But the Church of England espied them from afar, and begged them to join The Club. They were heretics ; that sufficed : their admission was a matter of course : accordingly, admitted they were. To be sure, they held a few doctrines which the Church of England professed to anathematize ; but what could that possibly matter ? They hated the Pope ; and this was reason enough why two "Bishops," a Dean, and several clergy, should cross the water to embrace them. What could Old Catholics do, in return for such kindness, but acknowledge "Anglican Orders?" O comic act of gratitude ! They had passed their lives in laughing at those orders ; but now they found them suddenly to be true.

Thus we get to the root of the Church of England "rule of faith." And thus also we see that to disobey the Catholic Church is to proclaim the right of believing or disbelieving, without obedience to any living voice.

No one can possibly obey the Church of England, both because she professes herself to be fallible, and proves every hour that she is so. No one can obey a particular ecclesiastic, because he has no more right to teach than any other. No one can " obey the Bible," as it is called, because he is at liberty to interpret it for himself. In short, there is no one to obey ; and consequently there is no one to disobey. Heresy is therefore rendered an impossibility — in a most certain, if satirical, sense ; because since every man must be necessarily his own teacher, he can disobey no one but himself. " Disobedience to self" is the only possible heresy that is left for an Anglican Christian. And since the self that may be disobeyed is a compound of opinions, of false traditions, false history, false interpretations, ungoverned by any authority save that of its own will, or at the best by the private " reading " of eighteen centuries, it is a self which it is perhaps better to disobey, than to honour with too much esteem. Really, we do not know how to address ourselves gravely to the subject of the unity of Protestants. If unity consist in such savage separations, that even different names must be given to different sects (some one reckons 289 within the " twelve-mile circuit " alone) ; if unity consist in the belief in the Mass, as taught by the High Church clergy, and also in the ribald blasphemy and scorn of it, as taught by the extreme Low Church clergy ; if unity mean both the adoration of the Real Presence, and its total disregard or denial ; if unity mean the belief in priestly powers, and the contempt for the apostolic succession ; if unity mean the teaching of Dr. Pusey, and also that of the Rev. Mr. Ryle ; if unity mean an appeal to the Councils, and an appeal to private opinions ; if unity mean the whole Sacramental system as insisted on by many English clergymen, and that kind of Quakerism *plus* a Form of Prayer which is insisted on by about as many more ; if unity mean that clergymen of the self-same communion should call one another " ungentlemanly

atheists," and yet remain in mutual serenity ; in short,
if unity mean the most prodigious disunion that was
ever conceived by the human mind ; then we must
concede to the Bishop of Ripon that Protestants are
united indeed.   But, for our part, we do not hesitate to
say, that it is not possible that Christianity should be
true, if the Church of England is its only representative.
It is not possible that the Incarnation should be represented by a system, which, to speak vernacularly, is the
incarnation of division.   If the Sacrifice on Calvary
have no better *in memoriam* than that imposture which
is called a " Communion-table," we say that we more
than question the Sacrifice.   If the Divine Apostolate
have no better representatives than the reverend gen-
tlemen who are perpetually getting married, we say that
we think lightly of the Apostolate.   If the " one faith,"
which Christ died to teach, is that taught by the Bishop
of Ripon, we have no opinion whatever of its " oneness."
If a Christian " house of worship "—which is the anti-
type of the Jewish temple—is represented by a Protestant room, in which a gentleman gets into a box,
and preaches some prayers, and then gets into another
box and preaches himself, we say that we decline that
" house of worship."   If adultery and murder, persecu-
tions and schisms,connubial reformers and apostate
monks, are the credentials, or symbols, or founders, or
Apostles, of the New Sixteenth Century Dispensation, we protest that we scorn that Dispensation.   We
know what Christianity must be, if indeed Christianity be
Divine ; and we know what Christianity *is*, because we
have it in the Catholic Church ; but Protestantism is
no more like Christianity, than Salisbury Plain is like
the Garden of Eden.   It is the torn shreds of the
seamless robe of Christ,—an impossible and inconceivable anomaly.   Happily, the robe is not torn.   Men
may be in the Church, and men may be out, but they
cannot be both in and out.   A spiritual membership
they may indeed possess, if they be baptized, and in
perfectly good faith ; and they may be saved through

the teaching of that One Church, which it is their misfortune not to know, not to love. They have the
Scriptures ; for the Church has preserved them, and
through the Church alone do they possess them ; and
though they mutilate or misapprehend those Scriptures,
still they cannot help learning a little. They have
fragments of dogmas, which they have borrowed from
the Church, and which may lead them back, if they will,
to their home. They have the true doctrine of the
Incarnation, taught them by the Councils of the Church ;
nor have they been able to resist the Church's
teaching on the doctrine of three Persons in one God.
All that they have they owe to the Church ; and, as a
great man has said, " There is not a Protestant who
now talks bravely against the Church, but who owes it
to the Church that he is able to talk at all." There
cannot be a question that millions have been saved,
through the teaching of the Church they disobeyed.
But that obstinate determination which some Protestants
evince—that "pravitas hœreticorum" which they cherish
—places them in a very different position from that
of their innocent victims. They are guilty of recklessly
deceiving, as well as of " deceiving themselves." They
might know the truth if they willed. Any Catholic
priest is ready to instruct them ; to hear their confessions ; to ease their souls of that burden of sins which
" obtenebrates " the intellect and conscience. But if
they go on throwing dust into the eyes of their hearers,
having first tried their hardest to blind themselves, their
responsibility will be terrible indeed. " It must needs
be that scandals come ; nevertheless woe unto that man
by whom the scandal cometh." St. Paul and' St. Peter
have both drawn pictures of modern Protestantism,
which read like photographs in words. They are
pictures of half England at the present day, that half
which is negatively called Protestant. "For there shall
be a time when they will not endure sound doctrine ;
but according to their own desires they will heep to
themselves teachers, having itching ears." And St.

Peter says, " There were also false prophets among the people, even as there also shall be among you lying teachers, who shall bring in sects of perdition." He speaks of "promising them liberty, whereas they themselves are the slaves of corruption." And it is against the teaching of these men that St. Paul expressly warns us, where he says, " I beseech you, brethren, by the name of our Lord Jesus Christ, that you all speak the same thing, and that there be no schisms among you; but that you be perfect in the same mind, and in the same judgment :" just as our Blessed Lord, in His last recorded prayer, asked the Father that His Church might be "one;" for the very reason, so urgent, so irresistible, "that the world may believe that thou hast sent me." (We stay here to remark, that one result of modern Protestantism has been to put back the conversion of the heathen ; since the heathen are so scandalised by Protestant divisions, that they are prejudiced against even true priests.) The Apostles further speak of these false preachers, as " despising goverment," " hating dominion ;" a test by which we may familiarly recognise both the principles and the expositors of Protestantism. " These are fountains without water," says St. Peter, " and clouds tossed with whirlwinds, to whom the mist of darkness is reserved." And St. Jude adds that " in the last time shall come mockers, walking according to their own desires in ungodliness ; these are they who *separate* themselves, sensual men, having not the Spirit." And it is remarkable that whereas St. Paul granted pardon to the incestuous person, he would scarcely concede it to the heretic. " A man that is a heretic, after the first and second admonition avoid ; knowing that he—that is, such an one—is subverted, and sinneth, being condemned by his own judgment." Thus, anything more opposed to the looseness of Protestantism, to its " spiritual " luxuriousness and indolence, than the incisive teaching of the apostles, it is really difficult to imagine. " Protestants have skilfully converted the Bible," says an able Catholic writer, " into a huge code of self-indulgence;" and the speciality of the indulgence is found in the fact that its luxuries are "matters of faith." Protestantism is a system of "indulgences." The Church—if we may here hazard a pleasantry—annexes very difficult conditions to the gaining the smallest "indulgence;" but Protestantism has no condition at all, save only, "Pray believe what you like: if you can agree with me, you will most likely be right; but if you can not, then agree with yourself." And the laity take the clergy at their word, and proceed to invent their own religions. They adopt some individual creed; and then they run about to this preacher or to that, in search of their pet hallucination. With "itching ears" they listen to men, who begin by proclaiming their fallibility, and end by reviling one another. Then, suspecting that some kind of unity is necessary, and feeling that they cannot get it among themselves, they all combine to "protest" against the Church. They go in crowds to a *once*-Catholic Cathedral, to hear a Protestant Bishop hold forth on the "errors" of the fountain and source of all truth. Their own errors are of little importance. That they cannot know the truth on any dogma of Christianity, save only through the Roman Catholic Church, is not a fact which stirs their enquiry; but the "errors of Popery" any one can teach them, because they are of Protestant invention. It would be better that an Anglican Bishop should preach on "the errors of Protestantism," and point out to his hearers "the abomination of desolation," which schism and heresy have begotten. *That* is the right thing for *him*. The Church of England has reached its last stage of hopeless fatuity and disgrace; and the only chance for its members to escape blank nihilism is to come bodily into the Catholic Church.

T. Rodgers, Printer, "Hallamshire" Steam Press, Change Alley Corner, Sheffield.

www.ingramcontent.com/pod-product-compliance
Lightning Source LLC
Chambersburg PA
CBHW031822090426
42739CB00008B/1373